Common Dolphins

ABDO
Publishing Company

A Buddy Book
by
Julie Murray

VISIT US AT
www.abdopub.com

Published by Buddy Books, an imprint of ABDO Publishing Company, 4940 Viking Drive, Suite 622, Edina, Minnesota 55435. Copyright © 2005 by Abdo Consulting Group, Inc. International copyrights reserved in all countries. No part of this book may be reproduced in any form without written permission from the publisher.

Printed in the United States.

Edited by: Christy DeVillier
Contributing Editors: Matt Ray, Michael P. Goecke
Graphic Design: Maria Hosley
Image Research: Deborah Coldiron
Photographs: Corel, Minden Pictures, Photodisc

Library of Congress Cataloging-in-Publication Data

Murray, Julie, 1969-
   Common Dolphins/Julie Murray.
      p. cm. — (Animal kingdom)
   Includes bibliographical references (p.) and index.
   Contents: Dolphins—Common dolphins—What they look like—Where they live—What they eat—Breathing—Senses—Groups—Babies.
   ISBN 1-59197-308-2
      1. Common dolphin—Juvenile literature. [1. Common dolphin. 2. Dolphins.] I. Title.

QL737.C432M86 2003
599.53'2—dc22
                                                      2003056265

Contents

Dolphins

There are 37 kinds of dolphins. They live in oceans and rivers around the world.

Dolphins, whales, and porpoises live in water. But these animals are not fish. They are sea mammals. Walruses, sea lions, and seals are sea mammals, too.

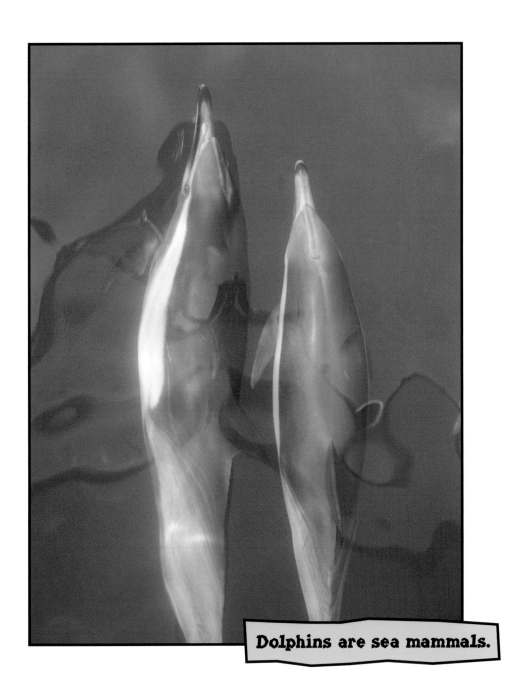

Dolphins are sea mammals.

Mammals use lungs to breathe air. Mammals are born alive instead of hatching from eggs. Baby mammals drink their mother's milk. Monkeys, tigers, deer, and people are mammals, too.

Most mammals have hair to keep them warm. Dolphins do not have hair. A thick layer of fat under their skin keeps them warm. This fat is called blubber.

Common Dolphins

There are two kinds of common dolphins. One kind has a long mouth, or beak. It is the long-beaked common dolphin. The other kind has a short beak. It is the short-beaked common dolphin.

A short-beaked common dolphin (left) and a long-beaked common dolphin (right).

7

Common dolphins are active and playful. They sometimes swim alongside ships. Common dolphins can do somersaults in the air, too.

Common dolphins live in large groups called herds. Some herds have as many as 1,000 members. There are also smaller groups within the herd. These smaller groups are called pods.

A pod of common dolphins.

Living in groups helps common dolphins guard against predators. Some predators of dolphins are killer whales and sharks.

What They Look Like

Common dolphins are long and sleek. They grow to become between six and seven feet (two m) long. Adults may weigh as much as 300 pounds (136 kg). Males are often larger than females.

Common dolphins are black or dark gray on their back. Their underside is light gray or creamy white.

Common dolphins have gray and yellowish tan colors on their sides. These colors form an hourglass shape.

Common dolphins have hourglass markings on their sides.

Common dolphins also have dark circles around their eyes. A dark stripe runs from their mouth to their flippers.

Flippers help to balance dolphins as they swim. Dolphins also have strong fins on their tail. These fins, or flukes, help them swim fast.

All dolphins have a blowhole for taking in air. This blowhole is on top of the dolphin's head. Dolphins shut their blowhole before going under water. They can stay under water for many minutes.

This dolphin is letting air out of its blowhole.

Where They Live

Common dolphins live in warm waters around the world. Long-beaked common dolphins usually live closer to shore. Short-beaked common dolphins mostly stay far out at sea.

Common dolphins live as far north as Japan and Norway. They live as far south as Argentina and New Zealand. Common dolphins live near the southern tip of Africa, too.

Danger to Dolphins

Over the years, millions of dolphins have died in fishing nets. Fishing crews accidentally catch them as they fish for tuna and other fish.

Today, many tuna-canning companies are careful about the tuna they buy. They do not buy fish from fishing crews that use dolphin-killing nets.

Eating

Common dolphins eat small fish and squid. They can eat as much as 20 pounds (nine kg) of food each day.

Sometimes, common dolphins in a pod will work together to trap fish. They swim underneath and around a group of fish. This makes it easier for the pod to catch the fish.

Common dolphins work together to catch food.

Common dolphins have more than 100 sharp teeth. They use their teeth to catch fish. But common dolphins do not chew their food. They swallow it whole.

Most kinds of dolphins have a lot of teeth.

Dolphin Sounds

Common dolphins communicate with each other. They do this through touch, movement, and sound. Dolphins make whistles, clicks, and chirps. Nobody fully understands what dolphin sounds mean.

Dolphins use sounds to find food, too. They will make sounds, then listen to the echoes. The echoes tell them the size and shape of what is ahead. This is called echolocation.

Echolocation helps dolphins find food.

Dolphin Calves

Dolphin babies are called calves. Female common dolphins usually have one baby at a time. Calves are born under water. Newborn calves are more than two feet (one m) long.

A dolphin mother helps her newborn calf swim to the surface for air. The calf stays close to her and drinks her milk. It begins eating fish after about six months.

Calves become adults by the age of four. Common dolphins may live to be 35 years old.

Important Words

blowhole the opening on top of a dolphin's head used for taking in air.

communicate to give and receive information. Talking is one way people communicate.

echolocation using sounds and echoes to learn the shape and size of objects ahead.

flippers the flat, paddle-shaped body parts that dolphins use to swim.

flukes tail fins.

mammal most living things that belong to this special group have hair, give birth to live babies, and make milk to feed their babies.

pod a group of dolphins that is smaller than a herd.

predator an animal that hunts and eats other animals.

Web Sites

To learn more about common dolphins, visit ABDO Publishing Company on the World Wide Web. Web sites about common dolphins are featured on our Book Links page. These links are routinely monitored and updated to provide the most current information available.

www.abdopub.com

Index